PERFORMANCE APPRAISAL

This book belongs to
Karen Duncan
Please borrow + read
but, Please, Please, RETURN

Rosemary Crawley is an experienced senior manager, who has been a director in a large housing organization. She currently works as a management trainer and consultant with a wide range of clients in public and private organizations.

PERFORMANCE APPRAISAL

Rosemary Crawley

GUIDES TO MANAGING DIVERSITY

LEMOS ASSOCIATES
LONDON

Published in Great Britain 1994 by

Lemos Associates
20 Pond Square
London N6 6BA

Telephone 081-348 8263

© Lemos Associates 1994

No part of this publication may be reproduced or transmitted in any form or by any means, electronically or mechanically, including photocopying, recording and information storage or retrieval system, without prior permission in writing from the publisher.

ISBN 1-898001-04-9

A CIP catalogue record for this book is available from the British Library

Cover design by Mick Keates
Phototypeset by Kerrypress Ltd, Luton
Printed by BPC Wheatons Ltd, Exeter

CONTENTS

FOREWORD	ix
1 INTRODUCTION	1
Purpose of the guide	1
Users of the guide	2
Benefits and caveats	3
Contents summary	3
2 PERFORMANCE APPRAISAL IN CONTEXT	7
Aims, outcomes and definition	7
Appraisal and performance management	9
Job requirements	11
Motivation	12
Plans, targets, values and standards	13
Performance-related pay	16
Equal opportunities	18
Positive and negative feedback	18
Training and development	19
3 EQUAL OPPORTUNITIES DIMENSION	21
Women	21
Black and ethnic minority people	24
People with disabilities	26
Lesbians and gay men	27
Summary	30
4 POLICY FRAMEWORK	31
Consultation	31
Policy contents	34

Purpose of the system	34
Access, use and confidentiality	34
Performance-related pay	35
Implementation expectations	37
Equal opportunities	40
Right of appeal and legal implications	41

5 PROCEDURE AND DOCUMENTATION — 44
Review of last appraisal	46
Purpose of interview	46
Identifying crucial issues	47
Identifying good performance	47
Identifying key targets	48
Finalising arrangements for interview	48
Self-appraisal by postholder	49
Postholder's review of job	49
Postholder's review of training needs	50
Reviewing other documents	50
Appraisal form	51
Continuity and review	52

6 PERFORMANCE APPRAISAL INTERVIEWS — 53
Preliminaries	53
Positive communication	54
Structuring the interview	57
Use of questions	59
Feedback	63
Using praise and criticism	64
Postholder's perspective and career planning	67
Concluding the interview	68

7 IMPLEMENTATION AND CONTINUITY — 70
Recording assessments	70
Action planning	71

8 TRAINING — 73
Performance appraisal system	73
Appraisees	74
Managers	75
Equal opportunities	76

9	MONITORING AND EVALUATION	78
	Monitoring	78
	Evaluation	79
	APPENDICES	83
	A Appraisal interview notification and checklist	84
	B Self-appraisal form	85
	C Performance appraisal form	87
	D Training and development plan	91
	E CRE code of practice	93
ACKNOWLEDGEMENTS		94
INDEX		95

FOREWORD

by Martin Willis

Staff appraisal is widely acknowledged to be an essential component of good management practice. At its best, it provides a means by which staff can be confident that not only are their current skills and knowledge being recognised by their organization but also that opportunities are being created for their future development and career progression. At its worst, it can feel like a means by which managers can pick faults with employees' work and set unreasonable targets to reinforce their authority.

To be effective, two requirements are necessary. Firstly, that appraisal should be conducted within the context of fair employment practices including clear and agreed job descriptions, equal opportunities policies which are implemented and monitored and procedures for consultation and complaint. Secondly, it needs to be seen as part of the staff supervision process, in effect a periodic evaluation of performance with future goals supported by training and regular reviews.

Rosemary Crawley explains how these requirements can be put into practice. She provides a discussion of the principles of effective staff appraisal with suggestions and models as to how these should be put into practice. Fundamentally, she argues that appraisal should be a shared process in which appraisees accept their responsibility to work to a standard consistent with the stated expectations of the organization and appraisers exercise their responsibility to be accountable for the performance of the staff they manage. Her book emphasises the importance of equal opportunities practice within this process – practice which empowers the individuals involved, sees difference as a potential strength and encourages managers to demonstrate equity in the way they identify and respond to good and bad performance.

Performance Appraisal has particular relevance for managers working in the wider spectrum of social care – housing, health and social services, statutory, voluntary and independent organizations. The book provides examples of the use of appraisal with staff of all grades, especially those involved in administrative and caring work whose needs for supervision, training and career development have often been neglected. Many organizations are now linking appraisal with the provision of training and assessment for NVQ and other awards, a development welcomed by lower-paid staff as tangible evidence of the importance the organization places on their contributions to the achievement of high quality service delivery.

Managers reading and using Rosemary Crawley's book will be stimulated to think about other creative ways in which they can use the appraisal process to help ensure the value of every member of staff.

Martin Willis
Director, Social Services Management Unit,
University of Birmingham.

CHAPTER 1

INTRODUCTION

Purpose of the guide

The purpose of this guide is to provide practical advice on developing and implementing a performance appraisal system. Examples of good practice in appraisal procedure and process are shown throughout.

The guide also covers ways of integrating good practice on equal opportunities into a performance appraisal system. The effective implementation of equality of opportunity within an organization should deliver an effective and motivated workforce for the organization. It should also make an important contribution to the career progress of individual members of staff, facilitating the full development of their relevant skills and abilities.

There is a growing appreciation of the value of formal performance appraisal in staff personal development. In residential social work, for example, serious performance issues have been in the public eye during recent years. The Staffordshire 'pin-down' scandal and Frank Beck's abuse of young people in Leicestershire –

both exposed in 1992 – raised important questions about the recruitment and supervision of staff. The report of the inquiry chaired by Norman Warner emphasised the key role of formal performance appraisal in bringing about significant improvements in staff training and development.

Users of the guide

This guide will be useful for:
— All managers who have to undertake appraisal interviews.
— Human resource professionals who are responsible for developing and implementing performance appraisal across the organization.
— Recently established organizations that are developing effective ways of motivating and managing staff within a clear framework of the organization's purpose, objectives and targets.
— People who are supervising and managing staff for the first time.
— Experienced managers who wish to establish a clear framework through appraisal for measuring individual performance against organizational goals.
— Managers with a responsibility for reviewing their organization's systems, policies, procedures or practice on performance appraisal.
— Trainers, internal or external, who provide training for managers or staff on performance appraisal.
— Staff who are being appraised for the first time.
— Those who are responsible for planning and for the translation of plans into objectives for individual staff.

Benefits and caveats

Performance appraisal, as part of a comprehensive performance management system, can make a significant contribution towards achieving a high level of motivation, performance and productivity. It may also contribute towards ensuring the retention of well-trained employees, and achieving better results from expenditure on education and training through continued evaluation of programmes, including induction training.

Performance appraisal forms part of a vital link between training and service quality, playing a role in the review of services in the light of changing customer needs and expectations. It is likely to assist staff in developing an appreciation of the organization's goals. Managers can become actively involved in helping staff to build on personal skills and self-confidence.

Performance appraisal is not without its difficulties. These have been sufficient to inhibit some employers from introducing it at all, or to create diffidence on the part of others in implementing systems wholeheartedly and with enthusiasm. The main risks and pitfalls are summarised in chapter 2 to enable managers to consider them in relation to their own organization. How they are resolved is inextricably linked not only to the design and implementation of the appraisal system but also to the degree of expertise and understanding which individual managers bring to the process.

Contents summary

Chapter 2 provides a definition and evaluation of performance appraisal. The importance of identifying the purpose to which the system is to be put is emphasised. There are several reasons why organizations adopt performance appraisal systems, and these will influence the nature and operation of the system used. The main reasons are described, and the inherent dilemmas which arise in systems intended to improve performance and those intended to inform future personnel decisions are identified and explored.

Chapter 3 discusses the equal opportunities dimension of performance appraisal. In particular it explores the implications for appraisal created by the continued disproportionately high representation of white men in senior management positions in most organizations. Topical information on equal opportunities in employment is provided, and the significance of organizational culture in the creation of a working environment in which people from diverse backgrounds can flourish is discussed.

The framework for the development of an appraisal policy and an implementation procedure is provided in chapters 4 and 5 respectively. It is important to clarify the role of appraisal in the overall context of organizational planning. The value of wide consultation in the process of formulating the policy is discussed. This contributes not only to the future effectiveness of the system through wider acceptance and ownership, but also facilitates the achievement of a sense of shared clarity of purpose. Appropriate methods of consultation are set out.

A clear statement of purpose is essential. It should include explicit reference to the use to be made of the information gained in the context of personnel management. For example, will it be linked to performance-related pay or other financial rewards? Does a 'good' appraisal imply promotion?

The policy itself defines the expectations of the parties involved, and the procedure, dealt with in chapter 5, will ensure a process which enables those expectations to be met. Here general guidance is provided in the course of discussing the procedural requirements. Also included is consideration of the preparation period together with specific advice on thorough and systematic preparation for both the appraising manager and the postholder, including the use of self-appraisal.

Chapter 6 focuses on the appraisal interview itself. Guidance is provided not only on structure but also on timing and control. This chapter also includes examples on the use of questions. Good interviewing skills are an essential prerequisite. Even experienced managers will benefit from regular re-evaluation of their practice in this area.

It is vital to treat each interview as a unique occasion, reconsidering each time the setting, issues for discussion and structure of the interview. This may appear self-evident, but without care, appraisal interviews may become routine. Every appraisal interview should be a discrete and special event in the working life of the postholder. Particular reference should be made to individual development needs and equal opportunities indicators, such as representation of women and black and ethnic minority people at senior levels within the organization.

Follow-up processes and training on performance appraisal are discussed in chapter 7. Efficient and competent follow-up after an appraisal interview is fundamental to the success of the system. The benefits to the organization and to the postholder will be abridged, and sometimes entirely negated if agreements reached and targets set are not consistently and conscientiously implemented. Well-phrased statements of action, and the precise identification of relevant personnel, as well as the need for clear communication systems with those who have a role but were not involved in the interview, are illustrated. The relationship between performance appraisal, regular supervision and on-the-job coaching is also tackled.

Managers require training in order to implement effective performance appraisal. An understanding of performance management as a whole is essential. They also need to communicate effectively in a variety of ways, identifying the appropriate communication medium for each occasion. Good written communication skills, the ability to lead effective meetings, and good interviewing skills; all of this needs to be complemented by the ability to plan and structure management activities and carry them out in a way which involves each postholder as an individual contributor to the organizational plan. The aspects of management development training required in relation to appraisal are outlined in chapter 8.

The guide concludes with a brief exploration in chapter 9 of monitoring and evaluating the performance appraisal system and indicates some of the areas which a useful evaluation might cover.

CHAPTER 2

PERFORMANCE APPRAISAL IN CONTEXT

Aims, outcomes and definition

The fundamental reason for carrying out appraisals is to improve individual postholders' work performance and therefore the performance of the organization in achieving its objectives.

There are other reasons and it is important to be aware of them, not least because they affect the procedures used and the nature of the information sought. These are: 1) planning individual development; 2) personnel planning, ie, deciding who to promote and how to reward people; and 3) workforce planning, ie, deciding how many people are required in the workforce and the skills and knowledge they should have.

Different procedures are needed to achieve these various objectives. Managers have to be clear at the outset about the use to made of the system. There is a significant difference in the approach to appraisals intended to improve performance, and appraisals intended to assist future personnel planning. In the former, the procedure needs to allow for extensive feedback to the postholder with a joint evaluation of performance, an outcome more likely to be reached by agreement. In the latter, feedback is likely to be limited, and evaluation will be undertaken solely by the manager. It is not realistic for one system and procedure to serve two such diverse purposes.

By contrast, appraisals to inform personnel action and appraisals to facilitate future workforce planning are naturally connected. One system could meet both objectives. There is also a link between appraisal to improve performance and appraisal to facilitate individual career development.

The systems discussed in this guide are intended to meet these latter two purposes, and at the same time, form an integral part of balanced performance management. So for these purposes performance appraisal is defined as the observation and evaluation of the work performance of an individual postholder set against known, agreed and measurable standards.

The manager is responsible for setting standards, communicating them to the postholder, and observing progress. The postholder is responsible for developing skills which will improve their capacity to meet the standards set, and communicating to the manager their experience and perceptions in the course of achieving them.

The interview process set out in chapter 6 combines and compares these two contributions, as well as providing for a joint evaluation of the progress achieved.

Appraisal and performance management

Effective performance appraisal is located within a comprehensive performance management framework, identifying the benefits to the organization, and the risks inherent in poor procedure as well as process. Such a framework is shown in diagram 1 below, with accountability at one end of the continuum and support and development at the other.

A comprehensive performance management framework incorporates all of the processes involved in ensuring completion of the tasks required to achieve the organization's aims. This begins with the accurate identification and description of the tasks. The next stage is to ensure that the best people are recruited to carry them out. (See also in this series: G. Lemos *Fair Recruitment and Selection*, 1994.) Once people are in post a range of procedures and processes are used with the twin aim of making employees accountable for the work they do, and supporting them in doing it.

In diagram 1, the position of each technique along the continuum is indicative rather than definitive. The aim is to achieve a balance between requiring accountability and providing support. A number of the procedures around the mid-point, including performance appraisal, incorporate both.

The art of management lies in choosing the appropriate techniques for the job in hand, and then employing them to achieve both accountability and support. Team meetings which focus on problem solving and supporting staff through difficulties to the exclusion of monitoring and reviewing performance targets will fail to emphasise accountability. On the other hand, individual supervision which is restricted to the presentation of work sheets and signed procedures may be so mechanistic and target orientated

Diagram 1 Performance Management Framework

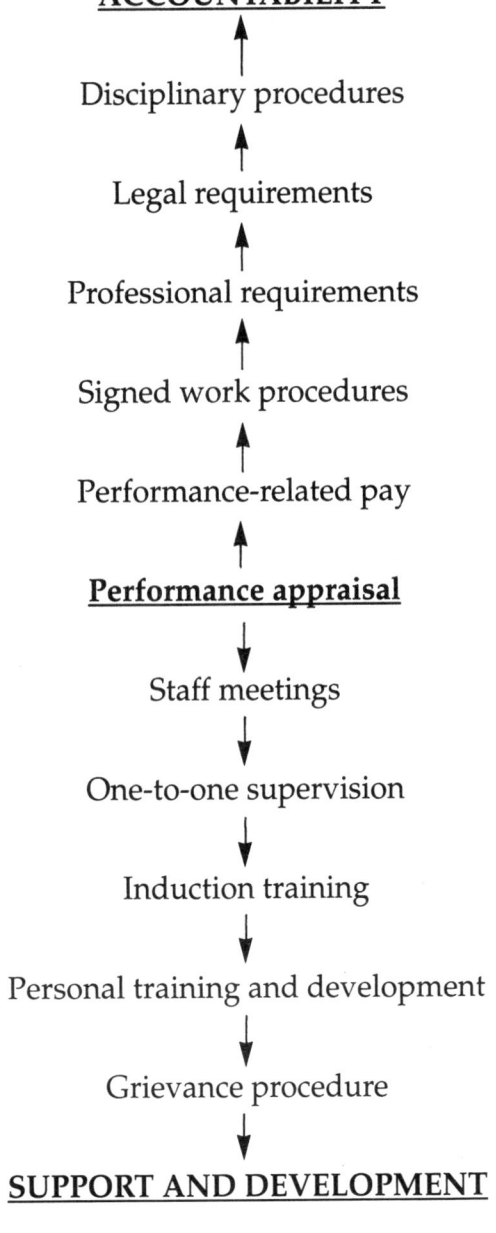

as to fail entirely to give support to individuals through difficulties, motivate them or set new or revised targets.

One role of the manager is to review and adapt the techniques employed regularly so that this balance between accountability and support is maintained. Performance appraisal interviews provide the opportunity for such a review focusing on the individual postholder.

Job requirements

The appraisal of actual performance against job requirements and standards can highlight any divergence between the two and indicate why this has occurred. The appraisal interview will look at the job from an overall perspective rather than at day-to-day details, which will be covered by other staff management techniques, such as individual supervision or team meetings already mentioned.

In the course of considering the reasons for a gap between requirements and performance, needs for long-term support may be identified. Support could be planned for both existing job performance as well as for new requirements which may arise in the context of setting new targets to fit in with the development needs of both the organization and the individual.

The appraisal interview is not the time to discuss extremely poor performance or poor conduct. It is not an alternative to a disciplinary procedure and should not be used as such. Any concerns about serious underperformance or poor conduct should be raised as and when they arise. They should be dealt with fully, and in line with the disciplinary procedure. Nothing in the interview should come as a surprise to the postholder.

This is not to say that personal traits which have an effect on performance cannot be discussed. There are times when these will affect performance. Typical examples might be rushing jobs at the cost of thorough attention to detail; or impatient or irritable responses to other staff, customers or members of the public.

Personal traits are only relevant insofar as they affect the postholder's behaviour at work. A positive discussion is more likely to ensue where the interviewer focuses on the behaviour in question, rather than on perceived personality defects.

Motivation

Motivating systems are ones which seek to inspire commitment, acknowledge achievement, provide opportunities for increased responsibility and promote a working environment which encourages creativity and intellectual development. Such systems will address the needs of each person as an individual, will include an equal opportunities perspective, and will balance accountability with support, as well as meeting the needs and objectives of the organization.

In his book *The Human Side of Enterprise*, D. McGregor comments on inspiring commitment:

> 'Commitment to objectives is a function of the rewards associated with their achievement.' ...
> 'External control and the threat of punishment are not the only means for bringing about effort towards organizational objectives. (People) will exercise self-direction and self-control in the service of objectives to which (they) are committed.'

McGregor also observes on encouraging creativity and responsibility:

> 'Under the conditions of modern industrial life, the intellectual potentialities of the average human being are only partially utilised.' ... 'The capacity to exercise a relatively high degree of imagination, ingenuity and creativity in the solution of organizational problems is widely, not narrowly, distributed in the population.' ... The average human being learns, under proper conditions, not only to accept but to seek responsibility.'

Plans, targets, values and standards

Definitions

The terms 'target', 'goal' and 'standard' used in this section have specific meanings. 'Target' describes the intended result of a work process. For example, in social care, a target may be to increase opportunities for independence of particular clients. This term is interchangeable with 'outcome'. A 'goal' is a specific step which goes part of the way towards achieving the target. 'Output' has a similar meaning.

The third term 'standard' describes the way in which work is carried out, and is closely linked to the values and philosophy discussed below. 'Standard' goes further and defines the time and expertise to be allocated to the task, together with other relevant conditions. For example, health service standards state how long patients must wait to see a doctor, the environment in which they wait, and how they are to be treated by staff whilst waiting, with particular emphasis on personal privacy and dignity.

Plans and targets

Both industrial and service organizations are regularly involved in planning in the context of management structures, markets, finance and services. The purpose of a corporate and business plan is to produce goals for the organization set in a framework of costs, timescales, values and standards. The plans will also indicate the skills required within the workforce. By also defining working behaviour – the way in which goals are to be achieved – values and philosophy become part of outputs and are thereby integrated into performance standards.

The appraisal system should ensure that individual workers are regularly and methodically re-directed in line with the organizational plans; also that their skills are updated, and, in some instances, supplemented to ensure a maximum contribution. Each member of staff should have a clear view of where the organization is going; how it intends to get there; and of their personal contribution to the process together with their personal targets.

Values

Organizational purpose can be translated into a task or, more commonly, a series of tasks. Different organizations bring to these tasks their own special philosophy and values. Public service organizations are likely to espouse values which uphold the civil and personal rights of those who benefit from their services. Industrial organizations are likely to espouse values concerned with the cost and quality of the product.

For the philosophy and values to be successfully applied in every aspect of the organization's work it is essential for every employee to understand the ideas, and how they affect the way in which their part of the corporate task is carried out. Performance appraisal provides an opportunity for this understanding to be fostered at an individual level. It enables an employer to promote corporate support and adherence to the values of the organization.

Standards

A salient aspect of planning is the projected description of the quality of the product or service. Through performance appraisal a description of this can be communicated to each individual worker. Effective performance management entails setting standards for individuals which support and progress the organization's strategic aims. In this respect appraisal forms an essential component of a quality management system.

The danger here is failing to be specific and precise. Standards must be achievable, logical and justifiable. They may be absolute or relative. They may be objective or based on subjective judgements. In areas of personal service standards may also be intangible. Where standards are subjective or intangible, it is essential to communicate to the postholder how they will be measured. For example, in a residential care setting, resident satisfaction should be one measurement criterion or performance indicator.

A further example of qualitative performance arises in the evaluation of staff supervision. The supervisee's evaluation may be based on additional or different criteria from those set for the supervisor. In order to take account of this, a tangible change or improvement in performance which can either be measured or described is likely to be the chosen performance indicator, as well as the supervisee's experience of supervision.

Performance-related pay

Performance appraisal is frequently used to inform decisions about pay awards and grading. Performance-related pay is considered in more detail in chapter 4. Where this link is made it should be stated explicitly in the policy. Organizations should also give careful consideration to the opportunities and difficulties which may arise.

The link to pay allows a clear connection to be made between achievement and reward both by the manager and the member of staff. It also provides the opportunity to reward excellence, that is performance which has not only exceeded expectations and targets set at the previous appraisal, but also has significantly contributed to the organization as a whole.

On the other hand, the connection between appraisals and performance-related pay may inhibit honest and open discussion of an individual's shortcomings. It may also lead to an increase in disputes about acceptable standards of performance. This may be exacerbated by the fast-changing technology of the modern working environment which often calls for workers to learn new skills and make major changes in the way they work. Without clear guidelines there may be confusion between ability to meet new performance criteria with ability to meet the original job requirements. This has the potential for actual or perceived unfair assessments.

One way to minimise these difficulties is to separate the performance-pay review from the appraisal interview by a period of six months. This separation should help to foster openness in the interview and provide time for the postholder to make the necessary changes in performance.

Risks and pitfalls

A lack of clarity about the purpose of performance appraisal will lead to defective implementation. Choosing an appraisal system which is open and incorporates full feedback to the employee may result in managers wishing to moderate the views and judgements they are prepared to express in order to avoid discomfort during a discussion. The effect of this on the value of the process needs to be taken into account.

It is further complicated where the system is linked to performance-related pay. Firm judgements on which to base pay and other career decisions are usually more successfully made in the context of a system which provides minimal feedback or opportunity for discussion.

Even where the system is for the sole purpose of improving and developing performance, employees may be suspicious about other uses to be made of the information gained. Performance-related pay has been topical in the media for some time. It is often presented as an intrinsic part of performance appraisal. The connection between appraisal and pay is best dealt with when producing the policy for the system and communicating it to the workforce (see chapter 4).

In carrying out performance appraisal, past performance should be assessed and future developments considered so that an individual and personal training and development plan can be produced (see also appendix D). To do this the manager must inevitably make a judgement about the relevance of current performance as an indicator of future potential performance. However misunderstandings can arise if this assessment is not kept separate from the discussion of current job requirements and the implications for future prospects.

The objective of making career progress may lead an employee to concentrate on areas of future development at the expense of current job requirements. A further risk is that the postholder gains the impression that promotion will automatically follow if the new skills that have been identified are successfully acquired.

Equal opportunities

Performance appraisal can provide a valuable means of promoting opportunities for individuals or groups who are often disadvantaged. Alternatively it may become a means of perpetuating and extending discrimination and oppression. Without careful thought and planning the outcome will be unpredictable.

Managers should understand that discrimination arising accidentally out of a poorly thought out and planned performance appraisal system is unacceptable to the employer and may be unlawful in certain circumstances. There is a responsibility to be knowledgeable and aware of those who often experience discrimination. This is a vital aspect of management training in achieving equality of opportunity in staff management practice as a whole, not only performance appraisal. It is discussed at greater length in chapter 3.

Positive and negative feedback

Giving positive feedback is the pleasant and easy part of an appraisal interview. It is therefore surprising how few managers seem to do it. A consistent complaint about performance appraisal is the over-emphasis on criticism at the expense of praising achievements. This is an important aspect of motivation and should not be omitted.

However, raising criticism may also be difficult, especially when it involves giving negative feedback. Failure to do this is likely to perpetuate poor performance by conveying the implied message that the performance is of a satisfactory standard. Often postholders will be aware that an improvement is required and may have prepared themselves to receive some negative feedback. They may also have the expectation that practical support in ways of improving performance will follow. In these circumstances, a manager's failure to raise the issue may cause an employee to feel at the very least confused. Guidance is given more generally in chapter 5.

When the postholder is black or from an ethnic minority group some managers may avoid raising issues, fearing allegations of racism. Unfair treatment lies in failing to raise the issue. Black people or people from other groups which are frequently undervalued may conclude that the issue has been ignored because they are considered to be incapable of changing their performance to achieve the required standard. Such a conclusion may lead the postholder to believe this of themselves and become convinced of his or her inferior capacities and dependent role (see also chapter 3).

Training and development

Performance appraisal followed up by individually planned training programmes makes a substantial contribution towards fostering equality. It constructively re-directs the individual towards increased use of intellectual potential, and towards integrating personal goals with those of the organization. This in turn creates an expansion of opportunities for the individual and benefits for the organization. A highly motivated, committed and skilled workforce results in a more effective and efficient organization.

Increasingly organizations are seeking to create and sustain a learning environment throughout their organization. As Tom Peters has observed:

> 'Throwing very smart, energetic people at problems is no longer enough ... a company's professionals must learn how to learn from one another, on the run and spread around the world ... Few ideas are more important (than the learning organization) and few have received so little practical attention to date.' (T. Peters *The World in 1994*.)

Appraisal has a crucial role to play in creating a structured, regular framework in which to consider learning needs and learning opportunities, and the successful achievement of that learning.

CHAPTER 3

EQUAL OPPORTUNITIES DIMENSION

Many job advertisements bear the slogan: 'We are an equal opportunities employer.' The concept of an effective equal opportunities employer within a society which does not offer equality in so many other aspects of life – such as education, housing, and health services – all of which influence individual employment opportunities, is, to a degree, inconsistent. Despite that, employers have a significant contribution to make to the quest for greater equality, and performance appraisal has a role in achieving it. This chapter discusses the employment experience of women; black and ethnic minority people; people with disabilities; and lesbians and gay men, and identifies the relevance of that experience to the appraisal process.

Women

Despite the large numbers of women in paid employment financial autonomy for them is still a long way off. Women remain largely segregated in the workforce. They are still represented in greater numbers as caterers or hairdressers rather than as surgeons or managers, for instance. Women's earnings are still substantially less than men's. Despite the aim of the Equal Pay Act 1970 to equalise terms and conditions of employment between men and women, there persists an overall gap of 23 per cent between the hourly rates of pay earned by full-time women workers and those earned by full-time male workers. (J. Rubery *The Economics of Value*, 1992.)

The Sex Discrimination Act 1975 makes it unlawful for employers to treat men or women less favourably on grounds of sex or marital status. Nevertheless, a number of practical barriers inhibit women's participation in employment. They have a disproportionate responsibility for caring for children and other dependents. They also are still disproportionately involved in domestic work.

These responsibilities frequently lead women into part-time work often with unsocial shift patterns. Women's need for this type of work to fit in with domestic responsibilities makes it easier for employers to limit the extension of benefits (such as company pensions or maternity benefit schemes) to full-time workers, and to pay different hourly rates to full and part-time workers, although discrimination against part-time workers in respect of statutory employment rights is not justified under European Community law binding in the UK.

Special issues for appraisals

The predominance of males in management roles is particularly relevant to performance appraisal. It will inevitably affect the appraisal process and so managers need to be aware of the effect of gender on the management of organizations. This is a wide-ranging topic which is touched on here. The male-constructed culture which predominates in most organizations creates dilemmas for women over how to behave. This often results in women adopting behaviour which they find unnatural in order to gain acceptance and make progress. This only serves to perpetuate the effect of the male power structure.

Conversely, women who are pursuing or exercising a powerful role and in doing so are acting assertively are often accused of lacking femininity. To avoid this women may resort to coyness or helplessness in order to seek to exercise power in a way they or others perceive to be more consistent with their feminine status. This perpetuates some of the stereotyped images which persist about women, and so makes it even more difficult for them to perform in a powerful role (see C. Cassel and S. Walsh 'Barriers to Women's Equality in the Workplace' *The Psychologist*, 1993).

Recruitment of women, or people with the responsibility for the care of dependents, to senior posts can be hindered by prejudices. These include the widespread assumption that such jobs must be filled by people who can work full time during conventional office hours or longer, and who will cultivate working relationships and gain information through traditional, that is male, middle-class networks and activities. It is not easy to challenge these assumptions whilst senior management in many organizations remains largely a white male middle-class preserve.

Wide appreciation of the benefits of change is required if significant progress is to be made. Changes in working patterns have advantages for both women and men. When these are appreciated in their own right – and not just as a mechanism for promoting equal opportunities – a step will have been taken towards valuing diversity rather than rewarding efforts to conform, whatever the personal and social cost. This step could lead to a more comprehensive understanding of what constitutes good management, in particular, an awareness of the different assumptions made about men and women in similar circumstances, and the effect of these assumptions on management decisions.

There are issues that may arise in performance appraisal where differences in gender may make the appraising manager inhibited or reticent. This might occur, for example, where sick leave had been taken as a result of gynaecological problems, and the manager is male and the member of staff being appraised is a woman. The structure of appraisal interviews allows difficult or sensitive issues to be addressed not in terms of the personal problems of the individual member of staff, but in terms of the impact on their job performance and ability to meet the objectives set. This should reduce the sensitivity of the subject and the difficulty of discussing it. In addition, effective interviewing and listening skills will be crucial to a non-emotive discussion focused on performance (see also chapter 6).

Black and ethnic minority people

In most organizations black and ethnic minority people are still under-represented in senior posts. Many years after the Race Relations Act 1976 the effects of historical domination remain difficult to overcome. The positive action provisions in the legislation remain comparatively under-used, and there is still a common misconception of positive action as positive discrimination.

Positive discrimination is giving preferential treatment to a group who have in the past been discriminated against. Except in very particular circumstances it is unlawful, and in any event, would be of little gain to the supposed beneficiaries. If people were given jobs because of their race, and not their abilities, however competent or able they turn out to be, they would always carry the 'stigma' of the reason for their original appointment.

Positive action, on the other hand, is offering encouragement to apply or training for jobs to members of disadvantaged groups who have in the past been discriminated against. It is legal, and encouraged by the Commission for Racial Equality, the Equal Opportunities Commission and successive governments.

Special issues for appraisals

In addition to the points previously discussed in chapter 2, black and ethnic minority staff who are managers may have other issues to resolve about how they treat people from a similar cultural background to themselves. Internalised racism – the persistent enforcement of negative stereotypes about black and ethnic minority people to the point that they themselves begin to believe those stereotypes or begin to behave as if they were true – may confuse black people who have succeeded in a white organizational culture. This sometimes leads either to denying or undervaluing the differences between themselves or others belonging to their ethnic group, and those of the dominant white culture. Put simply, they did not find the differences helpful to their struggle and they almost certainly (and probably quite accurately) attribute their success to their denial of those differences.

People with disabilities

The Disabled Persons (Employment) Act 1944 lays down minimum requirements for the employment of disabled people. Firms who employ 20 or more people are required to have a minimum of three per cent of their workforce who are registered as disabled. In addition, certain occupations (for example, passenger lift attendant and car park attendant) are reserved for people who are registered as disabled.

Although it is not an offence to be below the quota, if a firm is below quota, it has a further statutory duty to recruit suitable registered disabled people if any are available when vacancies arise. An employer who is below quota must not hire anyone other than a registered disable person without first obtaining a permit to do so. Nearly 17,000 employers below the three per cent disability quota were issued with a permit exempting them from their recruitment obligation in 1992-93 (Manpower Services statistics, 1994).

Special issues for appraisals

The appraisal system should meet the practical requirements of the workforce openly and ungrudgingly. The following quotation from Jenny Morris makes the point:

> 'It would mean a great deal to disabled people if, instead of assuming that the way our bodies work disqualifies us from employment there was a willingness to address the things we need in order to do a job. A failure to make buildings accessible, provide readers for blind people, sign language interpreters for deaf people, creates a life of unemployment and poverty. It also means that society is poorer for it loses the contribution we have to make.' (J. Morris *Disabled Lives*, 1992.)

Managers require a practical understanding of the effect of disability on those who experience it, and a consideration of the full range of practical steps which can be taken to make the workplace accessible and functional for disabled people.

Organizations need to promote an appreciation of disabled people as equal citizens with full civil rights including the right to participate in all aspects of society. Whilst some organizations have taken positive steps to facilitate opportunities for people with disabilities to join the workforce, most continue to see their disabled staff as dependents who should be grateful for the trouble taken to accommodate their needs. This maintains to a large extent their status as 'charity cases'. It falls far short of valuing them for what they have to contribute as individuals. In the context of performance appraisal it will inhibit the complete involvement of the person in the process. Unwarranted pressure may be placed on the person to prove that they are worth the money that has been spent and the trouble that has been taken.

Lesbians and gay men

Unlike race and gender, sexual orientation, generally speaking, may be concealed. When most gay men or lesbians start work with a new employer they form an impression of whether or not it is safe to make a statement to some or all of their colleagues about their sexual orientation and their lifestyle. Some of the factors which will affect that decision are:

1) The presence or absence of other out gay men and lesbians. A common phenomenon in organizations is that one person coming out leads shortly there-

after to several others doing so. This may happen many years after some or all of the gay and lesbian staff joined the organization.
2) The behaviour of other staff. If hostile remarks are common and go unchallenged many gay men and lesbians will conclude that coming out is likely to lead to harassment and it is therefore safer to say nothing about their sexual orientation.
3) The attitude and behaviour of managers in their own working practices and the way in which they deal with animosity or prejudice towards lesbians and gay men on the part of some or all of their staff.
4) The existence or absence of written statements of intent, policies and procedures about the needs of lesbians and gay men.
5) If the prevailing culture of the organization is one in which heterosexual relationships are held up as normal, endorsed, promoted and celebrated, while lesbian and gay relationships are either ignored or discussed as strange, disgusting or funny.
6) Lesbians and gay men might also experience the uncertainty of heterosexual colleagues – who may never have heard homosexuality openly discussed before, or mistakenly believe that they have never met a gay man or lesbian – as indifference or hostility. In fact it may be more akin to silent confusion.

Special issues for appraisals

Sometimes gay men and lesbians have come out at work without any particular problems. However, when they apply for promotion their sexual orientation is raised, questioning their suitability for the new post. This is prejudice and the only factors that should be considered are their skills, abilities and experience for the job for which they are applying.

There are circumstances where the prejudice against the newly-out lesbian or gay man is covert. Nothing specific is said. However the conclusion is drawn by managers and colleagues that this individual is not suitable for promotion. They may be thought too 'indiscreet', 'unreliable', 'flamboyant' or just too different. Often the true meaning of this reaction is that the manager, and possibly other managers, consider that the possibility of promoting a gay man or a lesbian is an assault on prevailing values within the organization. This may be so especially within the senior staff group where 'responsibility,' 'reliability', 'team-playing' are all said to have high premiums. Difference or dissent may be seen as a deficiency and, it might be thought, impossible to overcome.

This defence of existing organizational culture or values has also served to keep women out of the highest levels of organizations. Lesbians are therefore likely, because they are doubly different, to find themselves at a twofold disadvantage.

On the other hand, organizations will often reward risk-takers and people with initiative by promotion, though usually only when action has been within certain agreed parameters. Women, lesbian or heterosexual, black and ethnic minority people and gay men have found themselves chastised, even disciplined for taking risks which otherwise might have resulted in rewards if taken by a white man – someone seen as more conventional. It would seem that senior managers within organizations may tolerate and endorse risk in inverse proportion to the perceived 'differentness' of the person taking the risk.

Summary

Appraisal interviews should focus exclusively on job performance and the achievement of specified measurable targets. There is an opportunity for managers to be objective. Prejudices, either their own or those of others, some of which have been mentioned above, should not be allowed to get in the way of a manager's professional judgement.

An appraisal interview is also the occasion to explore the impact of prejudice and intolerance on the performance of an individual at work. In other more day-to-day discussions, an individual might be reluctant to raise these issues, but within the 'safe' environment of the appraisal interview they may feel able to do so.

Disability, colour, ethnic origin, gender and sexual orientation are all differences that are defined by comparison with the dominant white heterosexual male who does not have a disability. Appraising managers need to cultivate their personal awareness of the value of the differences within their workforce and incorporate the diversity it brings, rather than seek to maintain the traditional work style perpetuated by the dominant group. This means learning to appraise actual performance rather than a perception of it arising out of unacknowledged prejudice, or one based on a comparison with the 'way things have always been done'.

CHAPTER 4

POLICY FRAMEWORK

A performance appraisal policy statement is intended to provide a clear and detailed description of the appraisal system and what it is expected to deliver. The expectations of all who are involved in it should be plainly and comprehensively defined. It needs to be in line with other organizational structures and policies, including training, staff supervision, recruitment and selection, promotion and equal opportunities. The statement will also reflect the philosophy of the organization towards service delivery, customer care and personnel or human resources management. The role and limitations of performance appraisal in realising this philosophy will be described.

Consultation

The starting point, as explained in chapter 2, is to decide what performance appraisal is intended to achieve and to consider motivation and development as well as assessment and supervision. All of the organization's staff and managers have a stake in the appraisal system, not just the personnel section.

The next step is to decide who to involve in the design of the system. Performance appraisal makes explicit the link between individual performance, service delivery, training and career development opportunities, and so it is everybody's business. Consultation throughout the organization is also the key to the corporate ownership of a system to which everyone has had the possibility to contribute. This of course holds true only for a relatively short period of time after the initial consultation period and introduction of the system. Just how long depends upon the rate of staff turnover, and the rate and degree of organizational change.

To maintain this sense of overall involvement and ownership it will be necessary to carry out regular monitoring and reviews in a consultative style, with the additional objective of maintaining an apposite and up-to-date system. Evaluation and monitoring are discussed further in chapter 9.

Set out below are the stages that could be followed in using a consultation process within an organization.

Stage 1   Establish a series of discussion groups, each one consisting of a cross-section of staff including different grades, interests and occupations.
   Each group considers the need for appraisal and how present practice can be improved.

Stage 2   The conclusions of the various group discussions are collated and translated into an appraisal policy and procedure.
   This is presented to senior management and the trades unions or other representative bodies for further consultation.

Stage 3   The scheme is further amended in line with the second consultation and then operated.

This model may be varied to meet the requirements of different organizations. For example:

1) The senior managers have an input at the discussion stage (Stage 1) by providing options for consideration. This would be helpful in an organization where there is little existing knowledge or experience of appraisal.
2) Include in Stage 2 a pilot stage (say, for six or 12 months) prior to final consultation with senior managers and trades unions. The purpose of this would be to iron out operating difficulties early on and thereby facilitate a smooth introduction.
3) At some or all of the stages draw in an external facilitator to ensure that all of the 'stakeholders' are identified and have the opportunity to be fairly heard.

Consulting in small organizations

In small businesses or voluntary organizations a different approach to consultation will be required. The provision of basic information and training on performance appraisal may be needed before the consultation process can commence. If so, it could be helpful to involve an external consultant who can provide impartial knowledge. After this the consultation could follow the above model but with the involvement of the facilitator throughout the entire process. Staff should be assisted in airing concerns and discussing issues in a relaxed setting.

The following is a suggested brief when using external consultants covering three areas. First, the provision of a basic training course for all staff to ensure that there is a shared and common understanding of performance appraisal. The course should cover: definition; value; risks; and equal opportunities perspectives. Secondly, the facilitation of a planning day to produce an outline policy taking into account an assessment of the organization's particular requirements. Finally, the provision of training to senior staff in implementing, monitoring and evaluating the system.

Policy contents

The following is a checklist of headings to be included in a policy statement. The detailed contents are discussed below.

1) purpose of the system
2) use, access and confidentiality
3) performance-related pay
4) implementation expectations
5) equal opportunities
6) right of appeal and legal implications.

Purpose of the system

This has been covered both in chapter 2 and earlier in this chapter. It will not be discussed further here, other than to reiterate the importance of commencing with a clear, unambiguous statement of intent.

Access, use and confidentiality

A completed appraisal form is a confidential document. Whilst it should not be a detailed record of the appraisal interview, the form nevertheless contains personal and interview, the form nevertheless contains personal and sensitive information. It will describe successes, failures, aspirations and training needs. Therefore it is unsurprising that staff are often concerned about the use to be made of the document. Failure to provide unequivocal commitments about confidentiality sometimes results in the postholder being less candid, resulting in a less effective interview.

The statement should give information on where the form is to be kept and who is to have access to it. Access to information contained in the form must be restricted on a 'need-to-know' basis. The policy statement should indicate who is in this category.

Appraisal forms may be used to provide up-to-date information for references where the postholder is applying elsewhere for employment. This is a sensible practice which ensures that references reflect performance and that they are topical.

The information provided in this section of the statement may be reinforced by reference to, or brief repetition of the organizational policy about confidentiality of personnel documents.

Performance-related pay

Financial reward for excellence is widely regarded as a good idea. This is partly because of its perceived value in motivating people, and partly because it links expenditure and reward to output and quality.

For excellence to be determined it is necessary to set the standards, output and quality or outcome in advance, and to then to measure performance against them. This is not always entirely straightforward, although there are considerable benefits.

Service professionals

In some public service occupations, such as social work or nursing, far too simplistic an approach would be involved in the prior setting of standards and quantitative outputs. Many service professionals draw on a range of skills, knowledge and experiences, adapting them in response to a range of different circumstances. The outcome may only be partially determined by the way the job is done. Factors such as values, responses and behaviour of others (clients, patients, members of the public, for example) may all influence the end result.

This does not mean that it is impossible to assess the way such employees discharge their responsibilities. It certainly can be done, but a wider framework of assessment is required. Overall achievements need to be evaluated as well as individual tasks. The way the task is carried out is often equally or more important than the outcome.

To respond to this some professions have started to develop a framework of competencies – behaviour which demonstrates the possession of particular skills – which taken together are likely to improve the overall and detailed performance of the postholder.

Motivation

As outlined in chapter 2, there is a connection between motivation, commitment to objectives and the inherent urge to develop personal potential. This may become blurred and confused when the question of reward is also involved. The need for improvement arises not only from poor performance. At what stage do developmental requirements become actual job requirements and therefore assessable in relation to pay?

Linking performance appraisal to remuneration may result in de-motivation. For example, if performance is at an acceptable standard but not exceptional, no bonus may be paid. In these circumstances workers may feel themselves punished by the absence of an award. Too close a link between financial reward and appraisal may restrict the development of conditions where personal commitment together with the identification and realisation of personal goals can be achieved.

If there is to be a link, the two process should be kept separate. This will enable organizations to continue to maintain and develop other motivating factors. It will also give the postholder time to make any required improvements. Separation ought to ensure that the prospect of financial reward does not inhibit discussion of difficulties and challenges. Six months is a recommended interval between the two events.

Implementation expectations

A policy statement will set performance standards for the implementation of the system. This will include both operational standards and the longer-term expectations of the system.

Operational standards

The operational standards should include naming not only the managers who will undertake appraisal interviews but also the supervisory staff who will be assisting, either directly or through the provision of reports. For example, some staff such as finance or administration officers may have day-to-day contact with someone who is not designated as an appraising manager but who has a major role in setting targets for them, and in assessing their performance.

An individual may work inter-departmentally on a specific project or in an inter-departmental role giving more than one supervisor and manager a contribution to make to the appraisal process. One way of dealing with this is by convening an interview panel. This will create fundamental changes in the interview process. Potentially, it may place the postholder under stress, having to manage a number of different relationships within the one interview. To avoid this it will be necessary either to collect information from all of the supervisors concerned, or to hold a series of interviews involving the relevant supervisor at each one. The first option would seem to be the most helpful in reaching a rounded view, and is less cumbersome and time consuming.

Peer appraisals and appraisal by a combination of peers and managers are also options. Managers should seek to introduce variations which meet the operational circumstances of their organization.

Long-term expectations

Expectations of the system in the longer term relate to organization-wide concerns. For example:

— making the organization more effective in achieving its objectives
— ensuring that training and development of staff is more productive
— facilitating appropriate internal promotions of staff
— ensuring the equitable distribution of rewards.

Appraisal interviewing is complex. It is reasonable for staff to expect managers to have received training and to have attained a specified standard of performance. This is essential for the success of the system. The standard of interviewing and training are the fundamental underpinnings of the system.

The standards set should include: 1) the nature and amount of training to be undertaken; 2) the required detailed standard of performance in appraisal interviewing; and 3) a demonstrable understanding and appreciation not only of the value of a diverse workforce, but also of the needs of such a workforce during interviews. This will include a thorough understanding of the way in which people from groups who experience oppression and discrimination can be empowered in an appraisal interview.

Appraisal intended to improve performance in meeting organizational goals needs to be linked in time to the planning and review schedule. It also has to take account of the needs of individuals, joining at various times and stages of their careers. Some will have different skills or levels of skills. Others will have tasks of greater or lesser significance for the organization's goals.

Taking account of the needs of both the organization and of the individual, performance appraisal can be at its most effective when it is operated in conjunction with a one-to-one supervision system. In this way, monitoring can be maintained not only of motivation and progress towards achieving the targets and standards set in the appraisal interview, but also needs for training and support can be identified. Such supervision links new staff into the appraisal system from the outset.

Timing

New staff will benefit from a first appraisal interview three to six months after appointment. Then, depending on the complexity and nature of the job, the second interview could take place three to six months later. The more complex the job, its operating environment, and the speed of change, the more frequently appraisal may be needed.

Long-term employees or those in jobs with a high degree or routine and repetition will need interviewing less frequently; every eighteen months or two years may be sufficient.

The traditional 'annual appraisal' cannot properly meet this range of needs and differences. A flexible timetable is recommended with a minimum of six-monthly and a maximum of bi-annual intervals. Interviews taking place more frequently than every six months suggest poor performance which cannot be properly dealt with in the appraisal context. On the other hand, leaving interviews for longer than two years ignores the need for individual motivation, a reminder to the individual that they are needed and valued. It also risks failing to review the task itself and how it might be better performed to meet the organization's goals.

Equal opportunities

The policy statement should set out the organization's awareness of equal opportunities, referring to relevant policy requirements and acknowledging the diversity of the workforce. The statement should recognise and acknowledge the advantages that diversity in the workforce brings to the organization as a whole.

The statement should identify how it will meet the practical requirements of individual members of staff. For example,

'Access:

— involvement of advocates or supporters for previous or current mental health service users or persons with learning disabilities
— interpreters for deaf people
— readers for blind people.'

A further aspect to consider here is the media in which the policy statement is to be promulgated. As well as catering for people with specific communication requirements, many people who carry out essentially practical jobs, though they may have technically adequate reading skills, nonetheless do not readily absorb information from lengthy documents. Managers should be imaginative and innovative in the way they disseminate information. For example, videotapes and audiotapes are popular and accessible to many people.

Training for those to be appraised is yet another way of disseminating information about the system as well as being a useful practice in its own right (see also chapter 8).

In promoting equality the policy statement should not only acknowledge the inequalities which exist within the organization, but also set out a strategy to be employed in the context of performance appraisal to minimise the effect of those inequalities. It is sufficient in the policy statement to indicate an acknowledgment of these factors and a commitment to address them in the way the appraisal is implemented and the interview process is undertaken.

Right of appeal and legal implications

Some appraisal systems incorporate a right of appeal against the appraising managers assessment, or against the targets set. This introduces third-party arbitration where a conflict has arisen. Such a provision risks encouraging a perspective on the appraisal process which conflicts with the objective of achieving a mutual assessment of performance and a mutual agreement on the way forward. Appraisal assessment is not akin to delivering a school report; the joint nature of the process cannot be too strongly emphasised.

The legal consequences of appraisal are likely to be more significant when the process is used to inform decisions about promotion and the distribution of rewards than when it is used to enhance performance. Opinions about performance are less likely to be the subject of direct legal challenge. However, appraisal records may be used as evidence in other employment disputes, including applications to industrial tribunals in dismissal cases. This possibility reinforces the need for accurate record keeping which is descriptive rather than judgemental (see also chapter 7).

There may be times when the expected outcomes of the appraising manager and the postholder are at variance. This will not often be the case, despite the fact that appraisal interviewing is likely to be the most difficult form of interview a manager undertakes, and despite the inevitable risks and pitfalls.

The interview does not take place in isolation. It will be influenced by the postholder's relationship with the manager at the time, as well as by other events and conditions in the organization. This should be acknowledged in the policy statement in order to keep a commonsense perspective and to discourage unrealistic expectations of the system.

Deficiencies in the interviewing skills of the manager can result in failure to reach agreement on goals and standards; unclear messages about performance; too much or not enough negative feedback.

A thorough understanding of, and training in the interview process is likely to prove a more effective insurance against unresolved conflict than the provision of a right of appeal.

An appeal against the outcome of an appraisal interview is, to all intents and purposes, a grievance against the appraising manager. It cannot be satisfactorily resolved within the interview process; it is most appropriately dealt with under the grievance procedure. (See also appendix E).

CHAPTER 5

PROCEDURE AND DOCUMENTATION

A written procedure translates the policy statement into a practical working guide. It describes the steps to be taken, and sets the time frame in which the process will take place.

A fresh approach to each individual appraisal interview as discussed in chapter 6 below, may conflict with the concept of a written procedure. The risk is either having too many stipulations which result in a rigid and inflexible process, or not having enough and thereby encouraging slipshod performance. Either way the outcome is unsatisfactory. A balanced procedure will be prescriptive enough to reflect the policy standards – timing, frequency, setting, performance and so on – but the process should be relaxed and flexible, encouraging managers to think through a pertinent individual style.

Excessive documentation is not helpful. There should be a balance between too much information which duplicates the policy statement, and sufficient detail to ensure that the objectives of the policy statement are achieved.

The procedure will also set operational standards against which the system can be measured. Performance appraisal as a management function should be monitored against standards set both as a system, and on the performance of an individual manager.

The following checklist provides an aide-memoire on effective procedure.

1) notification of the intended interview date (see specimen form in appendix A)
2) preparation advice to appraising managers and postholders
3) an invitation to the postholder to indicate any particular requirements
4) the time and place of the interview
5) other documents to be referred to and how they are to be made available.

In large organizations the responsibility for producing and implementing the procedure will lie with the personnel section, whilst in smaller organizations it is usually the responsibility of the appraising manager.

Notification of interview date

A suitable and reasonable notice period for the interview is required. Depending on the organization, the post, and the individual concerned, time should be allowed for:

— any personal or practical requirements the postholder has to meet
— adequate preparation on the part of both the appraising manager and the postholder
— arranging cover for the postholder's work, if that is necessary.

Review of last appraisal

In carrying out this review the following key points will ensure that all aspects of past performance are considered by the appraising manager:

1) have there been any changes in the job content which should be discussed and acknowledged?
2) have the targets set at the last appraisal been achieved?
3) have the standards set at the last appraisal been achieved?
4) have the training and development needs identified at the last appraisal been met?

Purpose of interview

The manager is likely to have several objectives to be achieved during the interview, and these should be thought through.

It is probable that postholders will be at different stages of progress and achievement in various areas of their work. For example, it may be relevant to introduce to one postholder the idea that a new skill will be required in the future. Circumstances in which this would be appropriate are when parts of the job are to be computerised or when other new technology is to be introduced. The implementation may be some way off but introducing such new ideas in the setting of an appraisal interview where there is time to give full consideration to the implications for staff as individuals is prudent and a judicious use of the time available.

In contrast, there may be a need for another postholder to make greater use of a skill they already possess. For example, a supervisor of an expanding team may need to delegate in order to respond to an increase in demand for goods or services.

Planning the interview structure in advance is essential. It will ensure that the key issues are identified and that sufficient time is allocated to discussing them. It will also help the manager to identify a logical sequence for the discussion. This is not a call for a rigid and inflexible process. A good interview will incorporate the postholder's concerns as well as the manager's, and this in itself may change the planned structure. The existence of the plan will serve as a reminder to the manager of the issues to be discussed and will help to prevent the interview from drifting away into a general discussion. A suggested structure is set out in chapter 6 for use as a guideline. It is unhelpful to adopt any format for regular use without reconsidering its value on each occasion.

Identifying crucial issues

Is there an area of performance where a new approach is required? Perhaps a target or performance standard has not been achieved. Although this should already have been discussed directly with the postholder, ideally in one-to-one supervision meetings, the appraisal interview offers an opportunity for a fresh start with a different strategy.

Identifying good performance

Preparation time provides an opportunity to plan positively to avoid focusing only on criticism, whilst remembering the need for honesty. When evaluating performance the manager should look at the methods employed as well as the results. Even when the results have not been entirely satisfactory, the methods may be sound, indicating longer-term success and so worth building on. This added perspective has the advantage of extending the manager's consideration of the task beyond the immediacy of results to include behaviour and methods. It is useful in clarifying precisely what is being acknowledged as good performance.

Identifying key targets

A link has to be made between the postholder's future performance and the corporate or business plan together with the corporate ethos and values and the behaviour which reflects them. In essence this means identifying the unique contribution the postholder has to make. Having an appreciation of one's own value, understanding the contribution to be made, and the expectations to be fulfilled are key motivational factors. The postholder should have a clear view of what is required and the motivation to achieve it.

Finalising interview arrangements

The appraising manager must take responsibility for the interview setting. A comfortable, supportive and informal environment will be beneficial. This is not to suggest that the process itself is not formal or that a chat in the coffee room is the right approach. Formality is intended to equate with methodical and official, rather than with rigidity and strictness. The manager's aim should be to enable the postholder to participate in the interview with the minimum of inhibition. Consequently the manager's office is not usually the best place to achieve this.

The manager is also responsible for ensuring that the time allocated for the interview is uninterrupted. In organizations where there is a high-pressure working culture and where interruptions to meetings, training events and seminars are the norm rather than the exception this is of particular significance. An effective interview requires the undivided attention of both parties. The perceived importance of the process will be considerably enhanced if the interview is allowed to proceed undisturbed.

Self-appraisal by the postholder

There are differing views about to the value of self-appraisal. Some people are sceptical, in particular, when it is linked to performance-related pay. However, Dutfield and Eling in *The Communicating Manager* (1990) found evidence to suggest that individuals tend to be more critical of their own performance than their managers.

Self-appraisal can be useful on several counts. It requires the postholder to consider the interview in advance. Criticism by the manager may be more easily dealt with when the postholder has already identified weaknesses. Pinpointing what went wrong consequently could be speeded up and the discussion moved forward to exploring new strategies and techniques for the future. Finally, self-appraisal provides another perspective on the evaluation process.

Postholder's review of the job

In comparing the actual work against the job description the postholder should answer the following questions:

— are there any areas of the job description which no longer apply?
— have new tasks arisen which the postholder has taken on but are not acknowledged in the job description?
— why have these changes occurred?
— are the changes compatible with the objectives of the post and with the organization's goals?

Jobs may change in response to a number of influences. In the process of identifying those it is helpful to separate change into three categories, namely, new technology; the working environment including the needs of service users or customers; and the postholder's particular interests, expertise or limitations.

Postholder's review of training needs

A frank self-appraisal pinpointing achievements, aspects of the job that are challenging, and a comparison of the work with the job description will lead to a preliminary diagnosis of training needs. Various options for meeting training needs are discussed in chapter 8. See also a specimen format for documenting training needs and methods for meeting them in appendix D.

Reviewing other documents

The procedure should note the other documents which are to be used as part of the process. Among those included ought to be: 1) the performance appraisal policy statement; 2) the previous appraisal form; 3) a job description for the post; 4) supervision notes; and 5) the postholder's training record.

Managers who carry out appraisals infrequently, or where the appraisals are all bunched together in a short space of time during the year, need to refresh themselves on the policy detail. Postholders who do not themselves carry out appraisal interviews at all should re-read the policy before their interview.

Appraisal form

A specimen performance appraisal form is set out in appendix C. Design and layout is a matter for individual organizations, remembering the advice to keep documentation to the minimum.

Key headings for inclusion on a performance appraisal form are shown below:

1) personnel details (including name, post, date of appointment)
2) review of job
3) review of targets and standards set at last appraisal
4) review of training and development set at last appraisal
5) assessment of performance
6) new targets and standards
7) personal career planning
8) postholder's contribution
9) plan for monitoring and intended timing of next meeting
10) information about who sees the form. (A note should be included stating whether any senior manager, who was not present, may comment on the outcome of the interview.)

Continuity and review

The procedure will conclude with specific advice on how the outcome of the interview is to be implemented and monitored. In achieving this it will not only identify the relevant personnel and specify their role precisely, but also provide a format for monitoring and review (see also chapter 9).

CHAPTER 6

PERFORMANCE APPRAISAL INTERVIEWS

This chapter is intended to provide an aide-memoire to ensure that each appraisal interview is considered, planned and carried out afresh. The aim is to avoid becoming routine and to maintain a sense of purpose for each interview.

Preliminaries

The appraising manager's initial concern at the time of the interview is the comfort and well-being of the postholder. Choosing a suitable environment in which the postholder can best function has been discussed in chapter 5. Having achieved this, the preliminary stage of the interview requires the manager to extend to the postholder the usual courtesies and hospitality. This does not imply any special or different activities, but it is worth emphasising. In a work setting people who are usually courteous often overlook the gestures of hospitality which they would use naturally in other circumstances.

A few minutes spent in establishing the postholder's personal comfort and engaging in social conversation will be time well spent in easing any nervousness and establishing communication between the two participants.

Positive communication

It is vital to continue positive communication throughout the interview, even when difficult or contentious points are being discussed. To establish this sense the interviewer should adopt a comfortable and non-threatening position from which it is easy to maintain good eye contact with the interviewee. The interviewer will be listening for the majority of the time and should remain alert to the non-verbal messages they may be giving to the interviewee (see below).

Some basic ground rules on sustaining positive communication are set out below:

— sit facing the interviewee and on the same level as them
— a desk in between could be daunting (A coffee table might be more appropriate as there will need to be somewhere for papers.)
— interruptions during the interview should be avoided (Telephone calls should not be put through during the appraisal interview.)
— maintain good eye contact and do not gaze away into the distance or out of the window (Account should be taken, however, of any circumstances that make it embarrassing for a postholder to look someone directly in the eye.)
— do not fiddle with things (Have the papers required readily accessible, but refer to them as little as

possible, and refrain from repeatedly leafing through them. (Doodling should be avoided.)
— do not interrupt answers (Wait until the interviewee has finished before putting a further question.)
— having food in an interview is likely to be a distraction (A cup of coffee or tea may, on the other hand, lubricate the discussion.)

Non-verbal communication

As mentioned above, managers should be aware during the interview of their 'body language'. Such non-verbal communication consists of all the physical cues that people use to express themselves. These non-verbal messages are defined not by what is said, but by how it is said. Physical cues include eye contact, facial expression, tone and volume of voice, body position, gestures and the use of 'non-words'. So-called body language can either add power and force to what is expressed, or it can detract from or minimise it.

Verbal and non-verbal messages also needs to be congruent. If one message is given verbally and another through body language the listener will become confused. For example, if angry words are delivered with a smile or too timidly, the total effect will be contradictory. The intended message may be, 'What you are doing bothers me, don't do it again.' but the message received may be, 'She's joking, she doesn't really mind what I'm doing.' or, 'She's not going to do anything about it.' Body language should be honest and direct, to enhance the message, not to change or contradict it.

The questions set out below provide a checklist for the manager about how behaviour might be seen or interpreted by someone else.

Eye contact

Do I look the other person directly in the eye? Do my eyes shift away when talking? Do I lower my eyes when I am expressing negative feelings or saying 'No'? Can I give or accept praise or a compliment with full eye contact?

Facial expression

Can I keep my face firm when expressing angry or negative feelings? Do I find myself smiling when I am not amused or do not find anything particularly amusing? Do I giggle when I am feeling anxious?

Tone and volume of voice

Am I reluctant to use a firm tone of voice? Am I frequently ignored when I say something? Do other people interrupt when I am talking? Do I find myself appealing to others in a child-like voice?

Body position and gestures

Do I stand upright or slouched? Do I maintain an appropriate physical distance from people I am working with? Do I wring my hands, or fiddle with my hair, jewellery or keys? Do I sit forward or on the edge of my chair when I am anxious?

Active listening skills

Non-verbal communication not only affects what is said and how it is interpreted, but also has an impact on how things are heard. Managers conducting appraisal interviews need to ensure that they are listening, of course, but also that the person they are interviewing knows that they are listening. This in part requires giving clear signs of listening, such as nodding, or agreeing, or summarising or reflecting back to the person being interviewed what they have said, as well as maintaining eye contact. In addition it requires, as mentioned above, not being distracted by telephone calls, or pieces of paper being received during the interview, and not distracting an interviewee by fidgeting or doodling.

Listening skills are part of a wider framework of good practice in interviewing, and they are skills that will be needed in a number of circumstances. Their importance in appraisal however cannot be over-stressed.

Structuring the interview

The interview should be planned during the preparation period and a suggested structure is set out below.

First, the purpose of the interview should be clarified with the postholder; a shared perspective on this needs to be established at the outset. A restatement of the objective followed by an invitation to the postholder to set out their own expectations of the process would be a way to achieve this. It can be described as setting the ground rules, and reminds the postholder of the confidentiality of the interview and sets a time limit.

Secondly, the postholder ought to be invited to air any particular concerns and some response by the manager should be provided. If any issues relate to agenda points that have been noted for further discussion, a judgement is required about whether to discuss them at that stage or whether to point out that the item is on the agenda and will be dealt with later. Account must be taken of the degree of anxiety the issue is causing and the effect a decision to defer might have on the quality of the discussion in the meantime.

Thirdly, the interview agenda could proceed along the following lines:

- reviewing the work against the job description
- reviewing progress since the last appraisal interview (Have targets been met? Have standards been achieved?)
- reviewing the training undertaken since the last appraisal interview
- establishing new targets and standards in accordance with the organizational plan and the development needs of the post and the postholder
- identifying new training and development needs which will equip the postholder to meet required targets and standards
- identifying any other support the postholder may need, and discussing how it can best be provided.

Fourthly, the interview is best ended by 1) restating the agreements reached and the performance targets and standards to be met; 2) summarising the training, development and support programme identified and how it is to be provided; 3) explaining how progress will be monitored; and 4) agreeing a date for the next performance appraisal interview.

Timing and control of interview

An appraisal interview can degenerate into a ramble about the job, the organization or other irrelevant issues with no real purpose, and no outcome. Managers are usually conscious of the need to allocate a reasonable amount of time to the interview, but are not always clear on how that time should be used. They should keep the interview on course and not try to fill time artificially.

There is no ideal prescription for this. It will depend on the interaction of various factors. In particular the nature of the work being appraised and its complexity, and also the nature and range of the issues for discussion on each occasion. Provided that the interview is productive for both participants the time taken is not significant, so long as managers ensure that postholders do not feel devalued or shortchanged by a relatively brief interview. Generally, unless the issues were very complex or varied an interview should not take more than two hours.

Use of questions

The way in which questions are used is significant for the effectiveness of the interview process. Questions are asked either to establish facts or to explore issues in greater depth. They should be unambiguously phrased in a way which achieves their intended purpose.

Open and closed questions

Closed questions which indicate a 'Yes' or 'No' answer are useful for establishing facts. This kind of questioning has a role in appraisal interviews but it is likely to be a limited one given the exploratory nature of the process. For example, a closed question, 'Have you mastered the new filing system yet?' may only be answered 'Yes' or 'No'.

This is unsatisfactory for an appraisal because a follow-up question is now required. Bearing in mind that an interviewee should be speaking for most of the time, and that 'Yes' and 'No' answers inhibit the flow of exchange, a more appropriate open question would have been, 'How are you finding the new filing system?'

The postholder may respond with greater precision and include both positive and negative aspects without having to present a total failure or a total success. It also allows for comment on the system itself, as well as the postholder's use of it, which may be a useful addition to the information gained. An open question is more useful when a wide-ranging and comprehensive answer is sought.

Probes and reflections

In certain circumstances the flow of information comes to a halt. This may occur either when the postholder is unsure about whether further detail is wanted or where the postholder is describing an incident which has been experienced as difficult, embarrassing or distressing.

Questions which encourage the flow of information to resume and possibly which express a degree of empathy with the postholder's feelings are helpful. For example, '... And then what happened?' is a probing question which gives a clear message that further information is wanted. Alternatively, '... You must have been feeling quite angry/upset/anxious by this time.' is a reflective probe which expresses some understanding of what has been described without judging. This is likely to encourage the sharing of further information.

Questions to avoid

Questions should be short and restricted to one issue. Lengthy complex questions which incorporate statements are not helpful. For example, 'You will be aware of the new procedure introduced for monitoring staff sick leave. Have you had to use it yet and do you find it useful in reducing paperwork as intended? I expect you know that I was a member of the working party which produced it.' If the postholder can still remember the whole question, the answer may be, 'Yes. No. I don't know. Yes', but how helpful would that answer be?

The appraisal interview is not an appropriate time for promoting the procedure or explaining what it is intended to achieve. It may be pertinent to expand on either or both of those points later, depending on the initial response. Neither is it the time to draw attention to the manager's involvement in producing the procedure. That is almost guaranteed to ensure a less than candid response. A more useful question would be, 'How are you finding the new procedure for monitoring staff sick leave works in practice?"

Trick questions of any kind should be avoided. The use of excessively technical language, jargon, making personal remarks, sarcasm or mockery should also be avoided.

Hypothetical questions

A hypothetical question is unlikely to produce a response to a real situation and will contribute nothing to the development of work performance. For example, 'What would you do about it if you were in my shoes?'

The purpose of such a question may be to gain the postholder's support or sympathy for an unpopular decision. This is not a valid use of the appraisal interview. It may at times be useful to explain the reasons for a decision in some detail but it is never helpful to apologise for it or for managers to present themselves as victims.

Leading questions

A leading question limits the postholder's choice of answers in a way which will certainly restrict the usefulness of the response, and may set up hostility and resentment which will compromise the value of the entire interview. For example, 'Did you forget to switch the answering machine on because you were anxious to leave in time to catch the early bus?'

However the postholder answers this they are being led into admitting culpability in some respect. It would not be unreasonable to expect a hostile and defensive response.

Stereotypes and assumptions

In the interests of the promotion of equality of opportunity managers should take care to avoid invoking racist and sexist stereotypes and should avoid making assumptions based on their own personal values about the lifestyle of the postholder. For example, 'Couldn't your husband baby sit for one evening a week so that you could work an evening shift in future?'

The postholder may not be married or have a partner living with her. The dependent relative may not be a baby. It may be an elderly mother or other dependent who requires personal assistance.

It is wise not to make references to the postholder's domestic circumstances in the context of the job itself. This may be more relevant at the point where the interview focuses on training and personal development options and career progression. Where this is the case the manager should explain the relevance and avoid intrusive questioning. If the issue of staff availability outside normal hours arises the manager should ask, 'Are you available to attend . . . on Thursday evenings?' Assumptions should not be made or reasons sought if these are not readily provided.

Feedback

Giving constructive feedback

For most people feedback, when constructive, is an essential ingredient of learning and developing. Set out below are some guidelines for giving constructive feedback.

First, responses should be timely. This means giving feedback as soon as possible after the event. Secondly, responses need to be specific. This means describing actual instances of behaviour and reactions, particularly choosing those that are alright and those that should be changed. Thirdly, responses ought to be descriptive. This means talking about the consequences of behaviour in terms of its impact on oneself and not being judgemental. Fourthly, feedback should be 'owned' by the giver. This means speaking for oneself and not for others.

Here is an example of feedback using the guidelines, 'When you kept pushing your point, I found myself being unable to contribute and felt as though there was no use trying to pursue my own ideas.' Contrast this with the following example which does not follow the guidelines, 'You should not push so hard. It is rude and it got everyone upset.'

Receiving constructive feedback

The staff being appraised should also be encouraged to ask for feedback. Some suggestions on how to do that effectively may also be helpful to them. Guidelines for receiving constructive feedback are set out below.

First, feedback should be requested. It is important to be selective and find people who will be straightforward. They should be asked to be specific and descriptive. If information to answer a question or to pursue a learning goal is needed, ask for it. Secondly, responses should be directed. This means people should be told about particular concerns and what kind of feedback would be especially helpful. Thirdly, the feedback ought to be accepted. Behaviour should not be defended or justified. People should be listened to and thanked. What is helpful can be used; the rest can be quietly discarded.

Using praise and raising criticism

General principles

How can the all-important balance between the use of praise and criticism be achieved? Managers should use evidence and not assertion. The evidence they have must be specific rather than general. This avoids the 'you-are-great-at-your-job-but' approach which immediately negates the positive comment without even identifying what it related to precisely.

A better course would be to express appreciation for valued skills, identifying clearly what they are and inviting some discussion of them. For example, 'I appreciate the way you deal with difficult clients in reception. I am thinking particularly of Mr M last week, do you remember? How did you go about it?' This will lead to a discussion where the manager may indeed learn something new which might also benefit other people in the organization. It will also ensure that the use of praise is viewed as worthwhile and motivating for the postholder and not as an introduction to criticism.

When raising a criticism it is equally important to be specific. For example, 'On two occasions recently you have experienced difficulty in responding to a customer in accordance with agreed standards. I am thinking particularly of ... and ... Why do you think this happened?'

The use of examples in these circumstances avoids denial and helps the postholder to focus on real events. It also avoids the risk of presenting an exaggerated picture. When specific examples are not cited there is a temptation to imply that problems arise all the time rather than on some occasions. This is also likely to produce a defensive and hostile response.

The manager's aim is to initiate a positive discussion on corrective action, not to score points on whose analysis of the issue is right. Giving precise information in the first place is much more likely to prompt a thoughtful and positive reply. The manager should concentrate on discussing behaviour not attitude. Reference to attitude can initiate endless discussions on what the postholder's attitude really is.

Whatever the manager may think it is impossible to prove, and in any event, how is it relevant? Rather the objective is to appraise the postholder's performance – what is done and the way it is done. This advice is an extension of the guidance to concentrate on using evidence. It emphasises in a different way the importance of being specific and precise.

In concluding discussions involving criticism the imposition of targets and strategies for change should be avoided. Postholders ought to be encouraged to identify these for themselves. For example, 'How do you think you can change this?'

Interviewee's choices

It may be necessary for the appraising manager to suggest one or two ideas for the postholder to consider and choose from. In this case, the postholder should be encouraged to adapt the chosen strategy for themselves. If there is to be a timescale in which the change is to be achieved, the postholder should be encouraged to set it. Where there are other organizational constraints on time the manager should point them out first so that the postholder can take them into account in reaching a conclusion. For example, 'Bearing in mind . . . when do you think it is realistic for you to achieve this?'

The timescale chosen by the postholder is not usually over-extended. It is more likely to be unrealistically short. If this is the case the manager should go through once more the steps to be taken to achieve the target and in doing so introduce the factors which lead the manager to believe that the timescale chosen is unrealistic. Something may not have occurred to the postholder and talking it through once more will enable a more realistic target date to be set.

Personal commitment is invariably a more effective means of achieving change than compliance with imposed requirements. Encouraging the postholder to take the lead in this is more likely to result in a commitment to action rather than an agreement to comply with an expression of good intentions.

Summary

The guidance provided here on the use of praise and raising criticism may be summarised as follows:

1) balance the use of praise with raising criticism (bearing in mind the need for honesty)
2) use evidence not assertion
3) be precise and specific
4) concentrate on behaviour not on attitude
5) aim for commitment not compliance
6) aim for actions not intentions.

Postholder's perspective and career planning

The interview provides an opportunity for the postholder to discuss their own experience of the way training, support and supervision are provided. It may be necessary for the manager to give the postholder some assistance in responding honestly to this opportunity, particularly if the experience has not always been a positive one.

It is difficult for some people to criticise their line manager or the organization in face-to-face circumstances, but it is worth persevering with this because it is one opportunity for the manager to get feedback. For example, the postholder might be asked, 'What do you find most helpful about staff meetings/ one-to-one supervision/ in-house training courses?'

This is an invitation to the postholder to give an entirely personal view and to have that view listened to and discussed. Besides that, the information gained may be valuable to the organization as a whole for planning or in reviewing procedures. The information may assist the manager to gain insight into the impact of their management style. It may also raise equal opportunities issues hitherto unnoticed.

If the manager is genuinely taken by surprise and is unsure how to respond to a particular problem, it would be wise to defer the discussion. It is best to make it clear that the point will be addressed but that time for consideration is required. If this happens arrangements should then be made for the resumption of the discussion.

Before reaching final agreement on a training and development plan the postholder should be given a chance to discuss personal career aspirations. An indication of an acceptance on the part of the manager that in the long term the postholder's plans may not include staying with the organization will go some way towards expediting this discussion.

However the organizational culture which is a necessary prerequisite for this degree of honesty cannot be created in the context of a single interview. If there are concerns about future prospects, promotions or redundancies then this part of the interview may prove difficult, at least. Where this is the case it should be acknowledged in the context of encouraging some discussion about why it is not being pursued.

Concluding the interview

It is as important to end the interview on a positive note as it is to open it constructively. The main points for future action should be summarised and then the interviewee should be asked if there is anything further they would like to discuss. This should be done sincerely. The manager should not start putting things away or getting up until it is clear there is nothing further to be said.

The interviewee should be thanked for participating and, if possible, a positive comment made about some aspect of the way in which they participated.

CHAPTER 7

IMPLEMENTATION AND CONTINUITY

The follow-up process starts at the interview and the cycle is completed at the next interview when targets set and agreements reached are reviewed afresh.

Recording assessments

Brief sentences should be used to note assessments of performance. These would describe actual performance and state clearly the changes that are required. The use of grades or one-word descriptions such as 'excellent' or 'satisfactory' is not helpful in an appraisal which is intended to achieve a joint evaluation of performance. There is also a risk that too much importance is attached to the grade, deflecting attention from future planning.

Written assessments need to provide a sufficiently detailed record to be useful. Any values ascribed need to be directly related to the task and should be explained. A further advantage is that they are more readily transferable to a new manager in the event of personnel changes.

Action planning

The first stage in the implementation of agreements is translating them into a working action plan for all the parties involved. An example is provided below in diagram 2. This sets out what is to be achieved, the timescale, and expected performance standards. It indicates the project's range and all of those who have a legitimate interest in how it is being carried out. Identifying other interested people at a later stage is not helpful to the postholder and may be the cause of resentment when their views on progress are sought.

An indication of clear timescales will assist a training officer to plan the training on occasions appropriate to the relevant stages of the project. In the example given, the reading material needs to be ordered immediately; the training on health and safety legislation needs to take place within the first month; and the training on consultation within the first three months.

Most appraisal interviews give rise to more than one target although some will generate a more substantial programme of work than others. In each instance the expected outcomes, performance standards, and the inputs required to achieve them should be identified and documented to provide an agreed implementation plan.

Logically, the next appraisal interview will be set at the point of expiry of the longest target timescale. Where there are complex performance issues or a rapid period of change however it may be necessary to set it earlier.

Diagram 2 Specimen Action Plan

1) *Target*
   — to review and update the health and safety policy in line with current legislation

2) *Timescale*
   — six months

3) *Performance standards*
   — to consult identified personnel affected by the policy
   — to consult the recognised trades union
   — to identify the implications of the changes for other organizational policies
   — to identify the cost of implementing the changes
   — to secure the agreement of the senior management team

4) *Training*
   — health and safety legislation
   — consultation processes

5) *Support and supervision*
   — progress will be reviewed and discussed each month at one-to-one supervision meetings with the appraising manager, and, after the consultation stage, at the management team meeting

6) *Responsible personnel*
   — postholder
   — appraising manager
   — training officer
   — management team.

CHAPTER 8

TRAINING

This chapter identifies the principle components for training in performance appraisal. A successful appraisal system requires the managers with responsibility for implementing it to be adequately trained, and to have attained a specified standard of performance. Also, staff to be appraised will benefit from training and be better equipped to participate in the process. The third element of appraisal training concerns the equality dimension discussed in chapter 3.

Performance appraisal system

Training about the system itself, and what it is intended to achieve is recommended for both appraising managers and appraisees. The purpose is to develop an understanding of the reasoning behind the policy requirements, especially the more controversial areas. Achieving this will lead to a sense of ownership of the policy, and a commitment to its promotion and implementation.

Staff who were involved in the production of the policy will already have this sense of ownership and commitment as well as a practical understanding of what the policy is intended to achieve. As time passes and personnel change it is important to maintain and evolve these attributes among the new people who join the organization.

Appraisees

An additional focus of training for staff to be appraised is to impart a practical understanding of self-appraisal if this is to be part of the system. This will involve exercises in self-assessment as well as practical information on the use of the documents.

A further useful component is the self-assessment of learning styles. This will complement the identification of training needs which takes place in the course of self-appraisal, together with the development of ideas on effective training methods.

Training activities can be imaginative and varied, and should more often reflect the learning patterns of individuals. A number of assessment models are available but the four learning patterns to consider are: 1) learning through training; 2) learning by observing; 3) learning by reading; and 4) learning through direct involvement. See also the checklist in appendix D.

Individuals vary in their response to each of these methods and it is worth helping them to gain an understanding of the best method or combination of methods for them. It is necessary to follow this up by ensuring the provision of a variety of learning options for people to choose from when individual training plans are being produced.

Managers

People new to management positions may not have been called upon to implement performance appraisal in previous jobs and may be diffident about doing so. In these circumstances a thorough understanding of the system and of what it is intended to achieve should form part of a basic introductory course.

Training about the system is probably the easiest component to deliver although it should not be entirely restricted to information giving. It is important at this stage to promote the idea and its practical benefits. That will require the incorporation of concrete examples of what appraisal can deliver for the organization, the individual, and the manager (see also chapter 9).

The topics to be covered by the training are:

— the definition and purpose of performance appraisal
— the appraisal policy
— the appraisal procedure and documentation
— the interview process and effective follow-up.

This latter element should be participative training with plenty of opportunity for role play and regular constructive feedback.

The training should incorporate an assessment process either within the event or at a later stage to give appraisers an indication of their competence and some idea of any further training requirements.

Some individuals will find interviewing skills easier to develop and practise than others. Much depends on other interviewing skills and experience as well as on the individual's interpersonal skills. For the inexperienced manager it would be helpful to arrange at least one appraisal interview where they are the appraisee. They might also sit in on one or two others (where that has been agreed with the postholder) to gain an appreciation of the range of discussion and of the interview structure.

Attendance at a one-off training event is not a sufficient basis to presume an adequate standard of performance in appraisal interviewing, and it is for that reason that an assessment is recommended.

A list of key functions on which standards in interviewing could be set and measured are set out below:

— preparation
— greeting and establishing communication
— outlining the interview structure and handling initial queries
— use of questions and opening discussions
— use of praise
— raising criticism
— setting targets and standards
— personal career planning
— action planning.

Equal opportunities

Appraising managers need to understand equal opportunities issues, and the way in which they may affect the performance of people from particular groups not only in carrying out the job, but also during interviews. The purpose of training is to extend the manager's understanding of the origins of oppression and discrimination and the context in which this takes place.

The training should encompass a comprehensive exploration of the role and status of people from groups which experience oppression and discrimination. In particular it should include an examination of stereotypical imagery which continues adversely to affect opportunities at work for people from those groups.

This training is fundamental to all good management practice and will generally form part of a separate programme. However it should still be an integral part of performance appraisal training. The issues should be dealt with explicitly rather than by implication.

CHAPTER 9

MONITORING AND EVALUATION

Monitoring

Monitoring the implementation of the system provides quantitative information. This is useful in its own right and also establishes a basis for evaluation. It will verify that appraisal interviews are being carried out: it is good to know that the system is working and that it is not slipping quietly into disuse. Information should also be available on the appraising manager's own performance, and as such provide a basis for assessment when managers are being appraised.

It is useful in identifying the degree of activity which the process is generating, for example, the effect is has on training or productivity.

Monitoring should be carried out continuously. In large organizations this will be done by the personnel section. In smaller organizations it is usually the responsibility of each manager to maintain records. These will be combined and reviewed in the management team.

Evaluation

Evaluation goes further than monitoring and seeks to establish the worth of the system in comparison with the objectives set for it. The process of evaluation should identify what has actually happened and then make judgements about what has been good and useful, and what has been bad and unhelpful.

Outcomes

This aspect will involve an awareness of unexpected outcomes as well as those which were intended. Sometimes these are valuable and sometimes they are not. The evaluation process will judge these outcomes in the context of an overall performance management structure.

In addition to enhanced individual job performance and general organizational effectiveness, listed below are the areas where improvements might be anticipated:

1) standard of service or quality of product
2) corporate subscription to organizational values and philosophy
3) understanding of performance management as a whole both by managers and by other employees
4) effectiveness of one-to-one supervision meetings.

The degree to which the appraisal process is dependent on the skill and expertise of individual appraising managers will itself have an effect not only on the outcomes, but also the way employees experience the process.

Questions for evaluation process

Some of the questions that evaluating a performance appraisal system would seek to answer are set out below:

- to what extent does the appraisal system contribute to achieving the purposes of the organization?
- is it enabling organizational targets to be met?
- is it facilitating performance to agreed standards?
- is it producing a motivated and committed workforce?
- are rewards being distributed fairly and in accordance with individual performance?
- does it enable training resources to be targeted more appropriately to meet organizational purpose and direction?
- what is the value of appraisal to individual employees?
- are interviews being carried out in accordance with the standards set?
- does appraisal enable individuals to respond positively to the challenges of the job?
- does the process contribute to the individual's perception of themselves as valued employees?
- are individual employees committed to the implementation of the action plans which arise out of the process?

These are the main effects of the system into which organizations may want to enquire by means of an evaluation. Monitoring is a relatively simple process. Evaluation is much more complicated and large organizations are more likely to have the resources and expertise to carry it out.

Methods of evaluation

Listed below are the principle methods of evaluating performance appraisal schemes. Some are easier and less expensive than others although all require knowledge and experience of the processes involved.

— questionnaires to staff on a random basis
— group interviews with senior managers on the effects of the process on the organization
— measuring the effect of appraisal on staff take up and attendance at, and benefits of training courses
— group interviews with trades union members and representatives on the effect on industrial relations
— monitoring the quality and standard of goods and services provided by the organization.

All of these areas are complex and will be affected by a range of factors as well as performance appraisal. It is in identifying these and taking account of them in the evaluation process that expertise is required.

APPENDICES

SPECIMEN HUMAN RESOURCES DOCUMENTS

APPENDIX A
APPRAISAL INTERVIEW NOTIFICATION AND CHECKLIST

To:.. From: Personnel

You are invited to attend ....

for your appraisal interview on...

at..

The interview will be conducted by ....

who will be accompanied by ....

Please complete the attached self-appraisal form before the interview and return to the interviewer by...............

To assist you both in completing the form and in participating fully and productively in the interview, please consider the following points:

1) Who are you directly accountable and responsible to?
2) What are the boundaries of your work responsibilities? Are your responsibilities clearly differentiated from those of your work colleagues?
3) If you are responsible for supervising other staff, are you clear who they are and what your precise supervisory responsibilities are?
4) Are you fully familiar with the standards set for your performance? Consider how *you* think you are performing in relation to those standards.
5) How do *you* see you yourself progressing and in what way can your appraising manager help you to further your personal aims?

Copy to: appraisal interviewer (together with appraisal form and job description).

APPENDIX B
SELF-APPRAISAL FORM

Name .... Department ....

This form is to help you and your manager get the most benefit from your appraisal interview. Please consider the following questions before the interview and make a note of the answers in the space provided. This will be a valuable basis for discussion during the interview. The form must be sent to your appraising manager no later than ....

What have been your major duties and responsibilities over the past 6–12 months	Appraiser's comments
What skills/abilities do you use on your job?	Appraiser's comments
What particular skills/abilities do you have which are not being made use of in your job?	Appraiser's comments

In which areas of your job do you feel you need more experience or guidance?	Appraiser's comments
Which parts of your job interest you most and which parts interest you least?	Appraiser's comments
In order to improve your job performance what changes could be made by: a) Your manager: b) Yourself: c) Other people?	Appraiser's comments
Other observations	Appraiser's comments

APPENDIX C
PERFORMANCE APPRAISAL FORM
(This form must be signed and returned to the personnel administrator no later than seven days after the appraisal interview)

1) **Personnel details**

   Name..

   Starting date with organization ....

   Post..

   Date of appointment to this post ....

   Department............................. Location..................................

   Date of previous appraisal..

2) **Date of appraisal interview**..

3) **Review of targets and training from last appraisal**

3.1)

Target objectives	Target date	Progress & evaluation
1		
2		
3		

3.2)

Training/reading etc	Target date	Progress & evaluation
1		
2		
3		

4) **Assessment of performance against standards.
Identification of targets** (*duplicate as required*)

Job description tasks	Assessment of task performed	Target performance and required input
1		
2		
3		

Appendix C 89

5) **Has the job changed since the previous appraisal?**
Yes/No (*delete which is not applicable*)

If so, please note the agreed amendments

Job description Ref. No.	Brief note of changes

6) **Other issues discussed**

....
....
....

7) **Postholder's Comments/Signature**

....
....
....

Postholder's signature .... Date ....

8) **Targets**

Summary of targets	Action by	Target date
1		
2		
3		

9) **Training and development required** (*See appendix D for details of training methods*)

Need	Methodology	Action by	Target date
1			
2			
3			

10) **Date of next appraisal**

11) **Signatures confirming acceptance/agreement of above**

Appraising manager .... Date...............

Appraising manager's supervisor....................... Date...............

Chief Executive
(management grades only).................................. Date...............

APPENDIX D
TRAINING AND DEVELOPMENT PLAN
(To be completed at each appraisal for all members of staff and reviewed in supervision sessions)

1) **Current post**

1.1) Skills required (from job description and person specification):

   1..
   2..
   3..
   4..
   5..

1.2) Skills already acquired:

   1..
   2..
   3..
   4..
   5..

2) **Training and development needs**
   Training need 1 (*duplicate as necessary*)

   ....
   ....

   Appropriate learning style. Please tick one of the following:

   ❏ attendance on open courses outside the organization
   ❏ attendance at in-house courses
   ❏ self-managed open learning from written material
   ❏ coaching by managers
   ❏ job shadowing an existing postholder
   ❏ other; please specify

   Timescale ....
   Resource commitment ....

Training and development methods checklist

The following list is designed to prompt thinking about ways to promote staff training and development. The process is not exclusively about formal courses though if appropriate, relevant NVQ units should be noted.

- in-house training course
- external training course
- conference and seminars
- presentation to other staff/management committee
- coaching
- running a training workshop
- supervising student/trainee
- membership of working party/quality circle
- research
- report writing
- job swops/job rotation
- projects
- deputising/acting up
- placement with other departments
- open/distance learning
- secondments
- reading.

APPENDIX E

Extract on performance appraisals from the Employment Code of Practice of the Commission for Racial Equality:

Para 1.18 It is unlawful to discriminate on racial grounds in appraisals of employee performance

Para 1.19 It is recommended that:

a) Staff responsible for performance appraisals should be instructed not to discriminate on racial grounds

b) Assessment criteria should be examined to ensure that they are not unlawfully discriminatory.

The Code of Practice of the Equal Opportunities Commission does not include an explicit reference to performance appraisals. Nevertheless, discrimination in these circumstances on the grounds of sex or marital status is implicitly unlawful.

ACKNOWLEDGEMENTS

The consultation model in chapter 4 is based on an original case study by Clive Fletcher in his book *Appraisal* published by the Institute of Personnel Management.

INDEX

Access
  equal opportunities, 41
  policy statement, to, 34–5
Accountability
  performance management framework, 10
Action planning
  implementation and, 71
  specimen action plan, 72
Active listening skills, 56–7
Aims of appraisal, 7–8
Annual appraisal
  traditional, 40
Appeal
  policy statement, contents of, 41–3
Appraisal form
  key headings, 51
  specimen, 87–90
Assessment
  recording of, 70
Assumptions and stereotypes, 62–3

Benefits of appraisal, 3, 79

Black people
  equal opportunities, 24–5
  positive action, 24 25
  positive discrimination, 25
  special issues, 25
Body position, 56

Career planning, 67–8
Caveats on appraisal, 3
Checklist
  interview, 84
  procedure, 45
  training and development methods, 92
Closed questions, 59–60
Commission for Racial Equality
  recommendations, 25, 93
Commitment
  inspiring, 12
Communication
  active listening skills, 56–7
  body position, 56
  eye contact, 56
  facial expression, 56
  gestures, 56
  non-verbal, 55–7

Communication—*contd*
  positive, 54–5
  tone of voice, 56
  volume of voice, 56
Concluding interview, 68–9
Confidentiality
  policy statement, 34–5
Consultation
  process, 31–3
  small organization, 33–4
Contents summary, 3–6
Continuity and review, 52, 70–2
Control of interview, 58–9
Creativity
  encouraging, 13
Criticism and praise
  general principles, 64–6
  interviewee's choices, 66
  summary, 67

Date
  interview, notification of, 45 84
Definition of appraisal, 7–8
Development
  checklist, 92
  generally, 19–20
  performance management
    framework, 10
  plan, 91
Disabled people
  equal opportunities, 26–7
  minimum requirements for, 26
  special issues, 26–7
Disciplinary procedure
  appraisal interview not
    alternative to, 11
Documentation
  appraisal form, 51
  excessive, 44
  generally, 44–5
  human resources documents,
    84–92
  review of other documents, 50–1

Earnings
  women, of, 22
Equal opportunities
  black people,
    generally, 24–5
    special issues, 25
  disabled people,
    generally, 26
    special issues, 26–7
  gay men,
    generally, 27–8
    special issues, 28–9
  generally, 18, 21
  lesbians,
    generally, 27–8
    special issues, 28–9
  policy statement, contents of,
    40–1
  summary, 30
  training, 76–7
  women,
    generally, 21–2
    special issues, 22–4
Equal Opportunities Commission
  recommendations, 25, 93
Ethnic minority people
  equal opportunities, 24–5
  positive action, 24 25
  positive discrimination, 25
  special issues, 25
Evaluation
  methods of, 81
  outcomes, 79
  process of, 79
  questions relating to, 80
Eye contact, 56

Facial expression, 56
Feedback
  constructive,
    giving, 63
    receiving, 64
  negative, 19
  positive, 18–19

Finalising interview
 arrangements, 48-9

Gay men
 coming out, factors affecting
  decision on, 27-8
 equal opportunities, 27-9
 special issues, 28-9
Gestures, 56
Goal
 meaning, 13
Good performance
 identification of, 47-8
Guide
 contents summary, 3-6
 purpose, 1-2
 users of, 2

Human resources documents,
 84-92
Hypothetical questions, 61

Identification
 crucial issues, of, 47
 good performance, of, 47-8
 key targets, of, 48
Implementation
 action planning, 71-2
 long-term expectations, 38-9
 operational standards, 37-8
 policy statement, contents of,
  37-40
 recording assessments, 70
 specimen action plan, 72
 timing, 39-40
Individual development
 planning, 7
Industrial organization
 values of, 14
Interview
 active listening skills, 56-7

Interview—*contd*
 assumptions, 62-3
 body position, 56
 career planning and postholder,
  67-8
 checklist, 84
 communication,
  active listening skills, 56-7
  body position, 56
  eye contact, 56
  facial expression, 56
  gestures, 56
  non-verbal, 55-7
  positive, 54-5
  tone of voice, 56
  volume of voice, 56
 concluding, 68-9
 constructive feedback,
  giving, 63
  receiving, 64
 control of, 58-9
 date, notification of, 45 84
 eye contact, 56
 facial expression, 56
 feedback, 63-4
 finalising arrangements, 48-9
 generally, 53
 gestures, 56
 non-verbal communication,
  55-7
 positive communication, 54-5
 postholder's perspective, 67-8
 praise and criticism,
  general principles, 64-6
  interviewee's choices, 66
  summary, 67
 preliminaries, 53-4
 purpose of, 46-7
 questions,
  avoidable, 60-1
  closed, 59-60
  hypothetical, 61
  leading, 62
  open, 59-60
  probes, 60

Interview—*contd*
  questions—*contd*
    reflections, 60
    use of, 59–63
    stereotypes, 62–3
    structuring, 57–9
    timing, 58–9
    tone of voice, 56
    volume of voice, 56

Job
  actual performance, appraisal of, 11–12
  postholder's review of, 49–50

Last appraisal
  review of, 46
Leading questions, 62
Lesbians
  coming out, factors affecting decision on, 27–8
  equal opportunities, 27–9
  special issues, 28–9
Listening skills, 56–7
Long-term expectations
  implementation, 38–9

Management. *See* Performance management
Managers
  training, 75–6
Monitoring, 78
Motivation
  policy statement, contents of, 36–7
  systems, 12–13

Negative feedback
  effect of, 19
Non-verbal communication, 55–7

Notification of interview date, 45, 84
Nursing
  policy statement, contents of, 36

Open questions, 59–60
Operational standards
  implementation, 37–8
Outcomes of appraisal, 7–8, 79

Part-time work
  women, 22
Pay. *See* Performance-related pay
Performance appraisal
  aims, 7–8
  benefits, 3
  caveats, 3
  form, 51 87–90
  meaning, 7–8
  outcomes, 7–8
  purpose of guide, 1–2
  training. *See* Training
  users of guide, 2
Performance management
  appraisal as part of, 9–11
  framework, 10
Performance standards
  specimen action plan, 72
Performance-related pay
  generally, 16
  policy statement, 35–37
  risks and pitfalls, 17–18
Personnel
  planning, 7
  responsible, specimen action plan, 72
Plan
  purpose, 14
Planning
  individual development, 7
  personnel, 7
  workforce, 7 8

Policy framework
  consultation,
    process, 31–3
    small organization, 33–4
    generally, 31
    statement. *See* Policy statement
Policy statement
  access, 34–5
  appeal, right of, 41–3
  confidentiality, 34–5
  contents, 34
  equal opportunities, 40–1
  implementation expectations,
    generally, 37
    long-term expectations, 38–9
    operational standards, 37–8
    timing, 39–40
  legal implications, 41–3
  motivation, 36–7
  performance-related pay, 35
  purpose of system, 34
  service professionals, 36
  use, 34–5
Positive communication, 54–5
Positive feedback
  effect of, 18–19
Postholder
  career planning, 67–8
  perspective of, 67–8
  review of job, 49–50
  self-appraisal by, 49
  training needs, review of, 50
Praise and criticism
  general principles, 64–6
  interviewee's choices, 66
  summary, 67
Probes, 60
Procedure
  appraisal form, 51
  checklist, 45
  continuity and review, 52
  crucial issues, identification of, 47
  generally, 44–5

Procedure—*contd*
  good performance,
  identification of, 47–8
  interview,
    date, notification of, 45 84
    finalising arrangements, 48–9
    purpose of, 46–7
  job, postholder's review of, 50
  key targets, identification of, 48
  last appraisal, review of, 46
  postholder,
    job, review of, 49–50
    self-appraisal by, 49
    training needs, review of, 50
  review,
    continuity and, 52
    job, of, 49–50
    last appraisal, of, 46
    other documents, of, 50–1
    training needs, of, 50
  self-appraisal by postholder, 49
  training needs, postholder's
    review of, 50
Public service organization
  values of, 14
Purpose of guide, 1–2
Purpose of interview, 46–7
Purpose of system, 34

Questions
  evaluation process, for, 80
  interview. *See* Interview

Recording assessments, 70
Recruitment
  women, of, 23
Reflections, 60
Responsibility
  encouraging, 13
Review
  continuity and, 52
  job, of, 49–50
  last appraisal, of, 46

Review—*contd*
  other documents, of, 50–1
  training needs, of, 50

Self-appraisal
  form, 85–6
  postholder, by, 49
  training, 74
Service professionals
  policy statement, contents of, 36
Small organization
  consulting in, 33–4
Social work
  policy statement, contents of, 36
Specimen
  action plan, 72
  human resources documents, 84–92
Staff
  supervision, 15
Standards
  meaning, 13
  performance, specimen action plan, 72
  setting, 15
Stereotypes and asumptions, 62–3
Structuring interview, 57–9
Supervision
  specimen action plan, 72
  staff, 15
Support
  performance management framework, 10
  specimen action plan, 72

Targets
  key, identification of, 48
  meaning, 13
  plans and, 14
  specimen action plan, 72

Timing
  implementation expectations, 39–40
  interview, of, 58–9
  specimen action plan, 72
Tone of voice, 56
Training
  appraisees, 74
  checklist, 92
  equal opportunities, 76–7
  generally, 19–20 73
  managers, 75–6
  performance appraisal system, relating to, 73–4
  plan, 91
  review of needs, 50
  specimen action plan, 72

Use of policy statement, 34–5
Users of guide, 2

Values
  application of, 14–15
  industrial organization, of, 14
  public service organization, of, 14

Volume of voice, 56
Women
  earnings, 22
  equal opportunities, 21–4
  lesbians, 27–9
  part-time work, 22
  recruitment, 23
  special issues, 22–4
Workforce
  black people, 24–5
  disabled people, 26–7
  ethnic minority people, 24–5
  gay men, 27–9
  lesbians, 27–9
  planning, 7 8
  women, 21–4 27–9

Lemos

GUIDES TO MANAGING DIVERSITY

Helping you to achieve organizational excellence with today's diverse workforce

- provides guidance for all managers – junior and senior – on best practice
- sets out the policy context
- concisely written for managers by practising management experts
- includes specimen procedural documentation

GUIDE 1

FAIR RECRUITMENT AND SELECTION
getting the right person for the job
ISBN 1-898001-02-2   £14.95 paperback   1st edition

GUIDE 2

PERFORMANCE APPRAISAL
getting the best from your staff
ISBN 1-898001-04-9   £12.95 paperback   1st edition

To order by post or for further information:

LEMOS ASSOCIATES
20 POND SQUARE
LONDON N6 6BA
TEL: 081-348 8263